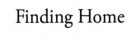

Finding Home

finding
HOME

Walking Surrendered Through Terminal Cancer and Failed Adoption

KIM GREEN

NASHVILLE

NEW YORK • LONDON • MELBOURNE • VANCOUVER

Finding Home

Walking Surrendered Through Terminal Cancer and Failed Adoption

Published in New York, New York, by Morgan James Publishing. Morgan James is a trademark of Morgan James, LLC. www.MorganJamesPublishing.com

ISBN 9781642798043 case laminate
ISBN 9781642798050 eBook
Library of Congress Control Number: 2019949873

Cover Design by:
Rachel Lopez
www.r2cdesign.com

Interior Design by:
Chris Treccani
www.3dogcreative.net

Morgan James is a proud partner of Habitat for Humanity Peninsula and Greater Williamsburg. Partners in building since 2006.

Get involved today! Visit
MorganJamesPublishing.com/giving-back

To you, Jodie, Jackson, and Noel!
May God be glorified through your stories
on finding your ways home.

Table of Contents

Acknowledgments

I'm deeply grateful to my Author relations manager, Tiffany Gibson, and the entire publishing team at Morgan James for helping me get this story in the hands of the readers. Your passion for the written word shines brightly!

Many thanks also to my wonderful editor Angie Kiesling and her team for their patience and fine editing suggestions.

And special thanks to my husband, friends and family who gave me the encouragement and time needed to write.

Introduction

It was December 26, 2014, when our extended family gathered to celebrate Christmas. Ben, our twelve kids, my mom and dad, Jodie and her two kids were present. Jodie had been cancer free for six months since a small tumor was last removed and fifteen months since she finished chemo and radiation after her initial small cell cervical cancer diagnosis in April 2013. The previous month of that year, she had begun having a lot of pain and peeing on herself. After ultrasounds, exams, and ultimately a PET scan, the oncologist told her that she had stage four small cell cervical cancer. It's a cancer so rare that little is known about it, let alone how to treat it and certainly not how to beat it.

I was in the room with my mom and Jodie with the cross of Christ hanging on the wall behind the doctor as she said these words: "I can't cure this, but we can try to slow it down." I've never been physically punched in the gut, but those words made me feel that I had. I couldn't breathe. None of us could. How? Why? Jodie was only thirty-eight. She was a single mom with two kids. And how, with the cross hanging above her head, could the doctor say that there was no hope?! With Christ, there is always hope! I was so angry . . . and sad . . . and scared at what lay ahead.

After what turned out to be her last family Christmas dinner, we were playing games and Jodie poured herself a glass of Coke. I texted my other sister—who was out of state—that if I ever saw Jodie again with a glass of Coke, I was going to pour it over her head! Had she learned nothing? Cancer loves sugar. Despite my inward temper tantrum, we enjoyed a great Christmas together.

Later that evening after we both returned to our own homes, Jodie texted me that she had been doing a personal exam and found something that didn't look right. As we chatted, I told her, "Weird is better than cancer." I think in her heart though, she knew it was back. Four days later, she felt a big gush and started bleeding again. The day after that, a CAT scan confirmed that cancer was once again ravaging her body. This time skinnier, weaker, and more deflated of the hope that once stood boldly inside her, she would begin the fight again with recommended chemotherapy.

* * * * * *

Jodie had wanted to write a book about her fight with cancer. She was never very good at school, nor did she enjoy it, so between the fear of not being good enough and being exhausted all the time, she never wrote the book on her heart. The closest thing she last came to writing anything was an adoption reference letter. Right before she was diagnosed for the third time in December 2014, Ben and I announced that we were going to adopt two little boys in Tanzania, our fifteenth and sixteenth children. We knew when we said yes to adopting them that there was going to be a bumpy road ahead of us; what we didn't know was how closely Jodie's journey to her heavenly home and the hope of the boys' journey to a home in America would intertwine.

This is that story.

Please note that the names of the people on the Tanzanian side of this story have been changed so that the authenticity of the story could be told without unintended personal harm. Integrity in all things is something we hold dear. Changing the names allowed the story to be told in its fullness.

PART ONE:

———————

The Backstory

Chapter One

Foundations

Let me introduce myself. I'm Kim, daughter of the Most High God, wife for over two decades to an amazing man named Ben, and momma to sixteen kids. Yes, you read that right! Ben and my honeymoon fairy tale plans of a white picket fence, two incomes, and three to four biological blond-haired and blue-eyed children . . . well, God laughed at that. I'm sure He even patted my head and thought, *You are so cute Kim, but I have FAR more than that for you.*

A year after we were married, my husband and I set out to create a family the old-fashioned way. Ben wanted three kids. I wanted four. We both grew up the oldest of three kids and each had two younger sisters. We had a lot of fun trying, but after a year, I still wasn't pregnant. Several doctor visits later, we were told we were infertile and the chance of us conceiving a biological child was pretty much zero. For several days, I cried my eyes out. I hadn't lost a baby through miscarriage, but it felt like I had lost all four of my hypothetical future children in some sort of horrific plane crash. I was devastated. Ben was numb.

Nine months went by of grasping at a few straws of fruitless infertility treatments and investigating domestic adoption. Neither felt right. Then, one day out of the blue, I asked Ben, "What about Korean adoption?" I had researched it and several other international countries extensively, ready for every rebuttal that he could throw at me. But he had none. We had unity for the first time since God told us no to biological children.

Well, those nine months of coming to the unity of saying yes to God's plan became a very fertile spiritual womb! Benjamin came home from Korea at five months old in April 2000. Kya came home from Korea at five months old in September 2001. After Kya, God spoke very clearly to me these words: "Not just the lost sheep, but the broken ones too." Before I had become a mom, I was a special education teacher. It seemed very fitting and we were very quickly drawn to a little boy with special needs who became our Parker. He came home a day shy of his second birthday in November 2002. In February 2004, McKenna, also with special needs, joined our family from Korea at eleven months old. Eli, with a few more special needs, made his appearance in our family in February 2005. By all accounts, I had just had five babies in less than five years! I told you I became very fertile . . . supernaturally so!

After Eli, we thought our family was complete, but I'm sure God was chuckling at me again. In October of that same year, I learned about a country in Africa that I couldn't even place on a map: Liberia. It didn't take long though and I was showing Ben waiting children. In May 2006, we brought home our only set of biological siblings, Caleb and Madisyn. We were told that they were one and almost three years old; however, Caleb was clearly older and was closer to five years old, which X-rays confirmed. As a result, we had his age changed in court.

The following April, I was in Korea helping my sister Melissa bring home my nephew—yes, I rubbed off on her!—and Ben kept receiving phone calls for domestic adoption situations. Back when we had received the infertility news, we had decided that domestic adoption sounded way too scary. We couldn't fathom loving a child and then having to give him or her back if the birth parent changed their mind before court. Something was different this time though. When I got back from Korea, I contacted our agency and told the adoption supervisor that we felt impressed to get our first domestic adoption home study. We knew that birth mothers usually choose families with no or few children, and so if we were hearing the Lord right, it had to be Him. We did. We heard absolutely right! A few weeks later in May

2007, we were on a plane to California and holding our first newborn, although eighth child, Liam. If you are keeping track, that is eight children in seven years. God had opened my supernatural womb, and it was pouring forth children faster than we could keep up with their diapers and sippy cups. I had the stretch marks to prove it!

The following summer we received a phone call from our agency asking if I knew any families open to a very special needs baby boy. I didn't, except for us of course. We weren't home study ready, and so we once again hurried up to do what we had become very good at doing: paperwork! At two months old, Isaiah joined our family from here in Michigan in 2008. The following May, I started corresponding with an adoptive mom who was looking for a new family for a little girl they had adopted the year prior from China. She had more special needs than they were anticipating as first-time parents in their later years, and they wanted her to excel, even if that meant in a new family. In June 2009, Klaire joined our family from Washington State at four years old.

Selah Hope was our next very special baby. She was born without a brain and lived a miraculous fifty-five days in the purpose that God had for her—one of which was to introduce her Muslim birth mom to Jesus Christ. In July 2010, we took her home from her Michigan hospital at eleven days old, and she died in my arms on September 12, 2010. We grieved her deeply because we loved her deeply.

Nine months later, in May 2011, God birthed into our family an expression of that joy He felt when we said yes to Selah . . . his name is Noah. Noah was born rocking an extra chromosome, and we like to say they still make good things in Detroit!

Are you dizzy yet?! I've almost got you caught up. Hold on a little longer!

May 2012 brought us another very special baby, Josiah, from Ohio, who was also born into hospice like Selah. We knew that his time would be short, so we loved him deeply until God took him home on April 1, 2013.

Four months after we buried Josiah, and we once again had the honor of saying yes to the Lord. Jonathon came home at five weeks old from New York and although he has significant special needs, he has far exceeded all doctors' expectations. The goodness of God is surely on his life.

Despite his overcomer attitude though, Jonathon has a lot of special needs and demanded a lot of our time and patience.

We thought for sure our family was complete at this point.

For sure.

Then God laughed at us again. We were called in great faith to pursue the adoption of two little boys with special needs in Tanzania. Jackson has albinism, and Noel has Down syndrome like Noah.

* * * * * *

You should know that God often speaks to me in dreams. That may seem weird to you, but if you look in the Bible you will see that God often spoke to people in their dreams. After all, God has a captive audience in the quiet of the night and the hush of our minds. He is able to speak spirit to spirit in the night hours.

He had forewarned me through a dream that we would adopt Klaire in 2009. She is autistic and honestly, that is the one special need that I had told God I really didn't want to parent. While I was still corresponding with her first adoptive mom, she had shared a picture with me, but she hadn't told me her name for confidentiality reasons. One night, I had a dream that I was driving down an expressway with cement construction barriers on the left side of my car. Suddenly, my car whipped around and was facing the opposite direction. Graffiti on the cement barrier spelled the name "Klaire." I know the difference between dreams from God and dreams from bad pizza because they are very clear and I wake up right afterward. God wants my attention when He does that, and He often gives me instructions, confirmations and strategies to solve problems. Well, the next day after my dream, her first adoptive mom told me her name finally: Klaire. It was spelled the exact way it was spelled in my dream. I knew she was ours, and she is.

In March 2012, I had another such "you are going to have a baby" dream. In the dream, set in an unfamiliar hospital, I approached a set of elevators but was told to go to another set. Only the invited could use these other elevators, which were staffed by an attendant. I got off on the fourth floor and was then instructed to go to bays three and four. I walked in and found a caucasian baby lying alone on a bed. I noticed that something was "wrong" with his mouth.

When I woke up I knew we were going to find out who our next son was and not only that, that after twelve kids, we were about to have our first caucasion baby. Sure enough, on April 3 (In my dream it was the fourth floor, bay three - which numerically is written, 4/3) I learned from several people about Josiah's impending birth. He had had two biological brothers born with the same fatal disorder on the cask gene. They had passed away in the previous years, and his birth parents just couldn't bury another son. We were asked if we could be Josiah's family until he went home to the Lord. It was our honor. Oh! About something being "wrong" with his mouth—I met him when he was only a few hours old and when I walked in (he was in bay three in the neonatal intensive care unit), he had a feeding tube in his mouth. Amazing God.

So, when I had another "you are going to have more kids" dream in fall 2014, I knew God was up to something again. The dream was very brief, but in it, I walked into a baby nursery where someone wheeled out to me black and white twins bundled up in blankets and in wooden cribs. I picked up the black baby, left the nursery, got into a four-by-four-type vehicle and tried to get on the entrance ramp to the expressway. I entered toward the bottom quarter of the ramp over the grass then got onto the pavement. After many frustrating attempts to get on the ramp, I eventually made it and was driving on the highway.

Chapter Two

Sisterhood

Earlier, I mentioned that I have two younger sisters. I was the oldest and wisest—okay, they might say the bossiest. Next was my sister Jodie, who was eighteen months younger than me. After her there was the baby of the family, Melissa, who is almost exactly four years younger than me.

We grew up in a two-parent working-class home. Our dad held various jobs from factory worker to custodian, and our mom stayed home with us throughout our childhood. We didn't have a perfect family, but it was a good family. We grew up close despite some financial hardship and personal failures.

Melissa and I were a lot alike. We both did well in school and received good grades. We attended the same college, have the same three teaching degrees, taught in the same school district, have both adopted, and after Melissa got married, we even lived within a block of each other until she moved all the way across the country.

Jodie was unlike either of us in pretty much every single way. We always joked that she was my dad in girl form. She was a tomboy of sorts, hated school, loved working in a factory, which she did—at the same one—for twenty years, was the only one of us girls to have biological children, and was married and then divorced two times. She never seemed to get ahead and was always striving to find peace.

While Melissa and I were close our entire lives, Jodie and I had our ups and downs. Our lives, and even some of our beliefs, were so very different that sometimes we didn't see eye to eye.

However, time, repentance, and prayer always brought us back together.

Sisterhood is a powerful force not easily broken.

Fast-forward to April 2013. Our son Josiah had just died, I had my fortieth birthday, and Jodie was diagnosed with cancer. All of this happened within just one month. Jodie had been having unusual pain in her "womanly area" and was all of a sudden unable to control her bladder. After a series of tests, I went with her and my mom to the oncologist for the results. Jodie undressed in a small room plastered with diagrams of the insides of women. Among the diagrams and pamphlets was a ceramic cross hanging alone on the wall next to the sink. It was a Catholic hospital, and every room had the same cross hanging in it. While we anxiously small talked our way through the wait for the doctor to come in, I focused on that cross. *God, please.*

An African-American female doctor entered the room, sat down, and then looked Jodie in the eye. She said that she was so sorry, but she had a very rare form of cancer called small cell cervical cancer. Only about 100 people a year are diagnosed with it and because of that and its extreme aggressive nature, the doctor said, "I can't cure this, but we can try to slow it down to buy you some time." What?! How?! She was a single mom with two little kids! How, with the cross of CHRIST hanging behind her could she say that?! There is always hope! That's how my Bible reads! I was so angry. I needed HOPE! We all did.

For the next six months, Jodie underwent intense chemo and radiation. Melissa and her family came up from their home in Florida, and we celebrated Christmas in July 2013. At that time, we took what would be our last whole-family photos. We didn't know how long Jodie had left and honestly, I think it cheered all of us up to have something to look forward to—just being together was good for everyone's souls. Because Jodie got so ill with treatment, she had to move back into our parents' home with her two kids during this time as well. So much humbling and transition took place in a very short amount of time. Jodie went from a strong "I can do anything" woman to a woman who could barely make it to the bathroom alone.

She finished her treatment in September 2013 and had another PET scan to determine what happened through that time period of chemo, radiation, and PRAYER. The whole time, I supported her choice of chemo and radiation despite what I saw it do to her body. She put her faith in the treatment. I was hanging my hat on CHRIST. I was praying and fasting and hoping that God had done the seemingly impossible.

Once again, my mom, Jodie, and I entered another examining room plastered with diagrams of the insides of women (God made us pretty darn amazing!), cancer pamphlets, and the cross hanging on the wall. It was now October 4, 2013. Anxiously, we waited and waited for the doctor to walk through the door. Jodie wore a yellow shirt and teal shorts (teal is one of the colors for cervical cancer); I wore in declaration my "On Earth as it is in Heaven" shirt; and my mom wore months of constant prayer, sleepless nights, and exhaustion on her sixty-five-year-old face.

Finally, the doctor walked in with papers in hand. It was her last day at the hospital as she had taken a job in another state. She sat down, smiled, and this time said, "These reports say that there is NO EVIDENCE OF CANCER IN YOUR BODY!" We all cried, and cried, and cried. We cried in the car. We cried at lunch. I cried on the two-hour drive home. I cried for days, and I'm crying right now typing this too! I don't know if I've ever been so THANKFUL in all my life.

Jesus won.

He defeated the grave yet again.

* * * * * *

Jodie continued to gain strength and health for the next several months, and in April 2014, she moved out of our parents' home and back into a place of her own a few miles down the road. She would still need help with the kids, but she needed to be independent again for her sanity's sake. She pushed herself hard and the following month started working again a few hours a night. She thought things were going well, until in July another lump was discovered in her uterus. The doctors felt it was contained though and could be resolved with a hysterectomy. Jodie was done having children so it wasn't really a big issue for her emotionally, but a few weeks later it would prove to be almost life threatening physically. The surgery was done robotically, and a part of her abdomen wall started collapsing into the space where her uterus had been. Thankfully God's hand never seemed to leave her, and she was as good as new once again after an emergency surgery and brief recovery.

Or so we thought.

In December 2014 she began experiencing alarming symptoms again, and that's where the synergy of this whole story really begins. Buckle up!

PART TWO:

The Walk Home

Chapter Three

Death and Life

In November 2014 I saw what seemed like a few random posts from an adoption agency starting a pilot program in the African country of Tanzania. Again, I must have failed geography in high school because it was another country that I had to go and look up on a map. As it turned out, Tanzania is in East Africa. The posts that piqued my curiosity were about two little boys about the same age growing up in the same orphanage. One was described as having Down syndrome and the other was albino. I thought, "They were black and white twins," although not biologically related! My spiritual bell went off. I emailed the agency for more information about the children and the country requirements. I was curious, and since we typically operate on the principle of walk until God shuts the door, what could it hurt?

As it was a brand new pilot program, they could only estimate when we might be able to adopt the children; they estimated less than a year and that both parents would have to make two to three trips to Tanzania. This is why God gives me dreams before His "bright ideas": So that I will agree to jump off the cliff with Him on these crazy adventures!

On my own, I would never choose international adoption again. The reasons being time away from our kids—we had never left the country at the same time—immigration requirements, paperwork, the huge expense, and the fact that it's just plain grueling emotionally.

At any rate, our "twins" names were Jackson and Noel, and they were both about three years old when we started the process. We had absolutely none of the money for adoption agency and lawyer fees when we started, but even right after Christmas people partnered with us and we raised the easiest $30,000 we had ever fundraised.

In other countries, including Tanzania, children with special needs don't have many options. Many are kept hidden, are killed, or are abandoned. Noel had been abandoned. However, his abandonment spoke of hope because his first mother left him on the steps of a Catholic church. She knew he'd be found and she knew, I believe, that whoever found him would do the right thing. That right thing included a call to the social welfare agency, which placed him in a baby home (orphanage) nearby.

Jackson's story was a little different. Upon his birth, he was instantly endangered because of his skin color. He was born with albinism. In several African countries, but particularly in Tanzania, persons with albinism are considered good luck and are mutilated and/or killed for their body parts. It seems like a story out of some archaic fairy tale, but it still happens today. Their body parts are sold to witch doctors and made into potions, which some people believe bring good luck. Sheltering a person with albinism, particularly in the area of Tanzania Jackson was from, also puts his or her entire family at risk of losing their lives. In fact, Jackson's mother reported that every single person in her village born with albinism had been killed and therefore keeping Jackson wasn't an option for her. Like Moses' mother, she hid him for as long as she could but the time came that she had to let him go in order for him to live. She made a twelve-hour bus ride to a larger city to do just that. Once there, she made a plan for him with social welfare that included what every child needs and she couldn't provide: safety.

Despite all of this, "I knew that I knew" that this was God. Ben and I have been married long enough that he knows when I "know" and he trusts me when I tell him that we "have to keep walking" until God shuts the door. This has proven true so many times in the past, and He has never failed us. We've started down paths toward kids out of curiosity, and God has shut the door on many. Every child with the last name "Green" was hand-chosen by God himself. You can be sure of that as the sky is blue.

So right before Christmas 2014, we announced that we were going to be pioneers in this new adoption program in Tanzania. With fear and trepidation, we were going to trust God and go down the path of making these boys, Jackson and Noel, our sons.

We had no idea what we were in for.

* * * * * *

Right after our "I can't believe we are doing this" announcement, Jodie received the results from her most recent CAT scan. Upon turning the page of the year 2014, on December 31 she was told that cancer was once again ravaging her pelvic area.

While we were celebrating the potential of two new lives, she was fearing death. Again.

Chapter Four

It is Well

There is a great hymn called "It Is Well with My Soul" that goes like this:

When peace, like a river, attendeth my way,
When sorrows like sea billows roll; Whatever my lot, Thou
hast taught me to say,
It is well, it is well with my soul.

Refrain:
It is well with my soul,
It is well, it is well with my soul.
Though Satan should buffet, though trials should come,
Let this blest assurance control,

That Christ hath regarded my helpless estate,
And hath shed His own blood for my soul.
My sin—oh, the bliss of this glorious thought!—
My sin, not in part but the whole,
Is nailed to the cross, and I bear it no more,
Praise the Lord, praise the Lord, O my soul!
For me, be it Christ, be it Christ hence to live:
If Jordan above me shall roll,
No pang shall be mine, for in death as in life
Thou wilt whisper Thy peace to my soul.
But, Lord, 'tis for Thee, for Thy coming we wait,
The sky, not the grave, is our goal;
Oh, trump of the angel! Oh, voice of the Lord!
Blessed hope, blessed rest of my soul!
And Lord, haste the day when the faith shall be sight,
The clouds be rolled back as a scroll;
The trump shall resound, and the Lord shall descend,
Even so, it is well with my soul.

The phrase "it is well" was burning on Melissa's heart and mine that December, even before the December 31 diagnosis of cancer again. The original hymn was written after traumatic events in Horatio Spafford's life. His two-year-old son had died, the Great Chicago Fire had ruined him financially, and then tragically, his wife and four daughters were shipwrecked, during which time his four daughters died. As Horatio traveled to Europe to meet his grieving wife and passed near where the ship went down and his children died, this song was birthed from his heart. He had hope in something greater than his circumstances to be able to declare it was well despite such great loss.

But even before this great hymn was penned, the Shunamite woman in 2 Kings declared "all is well" when her young son died unexpectedly. She declared those words all the way back to Elisha, who she then, in essence, exclaimed, "Fix this!" And with God's help, he did. These Scriptures would even become the context for a message that I had the opportunity to preach in our church. We believed them with all our hearts. It was well, despite our circumstances or the outcome, because God is good. It became the declaration of our hearts with each and every twist and turn of the next several months:

It is well.

* * * * * *

Jodie began chemo again in January 2015 and had surgery to put a stent in her urethra. The tumor was growing rapidly, putting pressure on the urethra, and they were trying to save her kidney by putting in the stent. During the first surgery on January 9, I drove alone across Michigan through the worst snowstorm I've ever driven through in my life. What normally took two hours took four. I was terrified, but my fear drove me to call on Him every second for four hours straight. After I picked Jodie up, we finally arrived at the hospital, and while she was getting prepped, it was realized that she hadn't followed the pre-op instructions. She had eaten within the six hours she wasn't supposed to, so the doctor rescheduled the surgery. Jodie was *so* angry. She cried to the nurse that she needed this surgery so she could start chemo. She could feel time racing against her. Cancer's sole mission is to devour, and she could feel the battle raging within.

This doctor who rescheduled the surgery was new to us, as Jodie's female oncologist who had given her the "no evidence of cancer" news in October 2013 had since transferred to a different hospital. To my knowledge, Jodie was the last patient she saw at that hospital. Jodie was then transferred to the only other doctor available for her type of female cancer. We will call him Dr. B here, but let's just say she despised him. My mom despised him as well. He apparently feared me, but I never met him except for a brief after-surgery report. His abrupt manner of conversation and lack of compassion made any news from him seem ten times worse.

Two weeks later, Jodie got the stent put in successfully and she began chemo once again by the end of January. The first two rounds of chemo seemed to be easier than the first time in 2013. She wasn't getting as sick and we were hopeful that something was working, except that wasn't the case at all. In February, she went to the emergency room for severe pelvic pain. I didn't rush over because a friend was with her and she wanted to make sure she didn't just get sent home. That was on a Saturday and during the course of the afternoon, the diagnosis changed a few times depending on who read the scan. By evening, Jodie was admitted and told that she'd be having surgery the next day to simply remove some fluid that had built up.

Sunday, February 22, while I was on the way home from church, Jodie called me. She was crying and was so angry about Dr. B's callous delivery of the most tragic news. She said that he had read the scan in front of her, evaluated the situation, and told her that she was terminal—that there was nothing they could do except make her as comfortable as possible. They weren't going to do anything further for her. She was devastated. I was numb. I remember exactly where our red fifteen-passenger van was when I heard those words. I also remember hardly shedding a tear as I just didn't feel this was the end. There was more to her story. The stubbornness in Melissa and I rose up congruently, and we started looking for different angles and more opinions in addition to the continuous prayer that was on many people's lips.

Melissa called up some connections she had at an excellent hospital in Michigan, and I went on the internet. A hospital in Chicago that I had never heard of popped out at me. It was late Sunday night, but I private messaged Jodie on Facebook with the link. I told her that they have a twenty-four-hour line and suggested she call. Much to my surprise, she did! She called me shortly after ten that night and the hope I heard in her voice still makes me tear up today. Immediately, I told Melissa and we started praying that Jodie could get a second opinion through this hospital.

A few days later, the details between the hospital and insurance company were worked out and Jodie asked if I'd go with her for a three-day evaluation. So often "we cry out for revival, and yet God says, 'I want to open your eyes so you can see what is before you. Revival has a face and a name. It lies bleeding on the roadside.' " (*Reckless Devotion: 365 Days of Radical Love*, Heidi and Rolland Baker) This time her name was Jodie. At that point, I committed to do everything I could to help her, no matter the personal cost.

It isn't easy for a mother of twelve to go away for a few days, but God is so good that He worked out every detail for everyone's needs to be met almost instantaneously. A missionary friend of ours who had been in Romania needed a place to stay for a few months while she transitioned back to the States. It just so happened that she was scheduled to come back the very same day I was leaving with Jodie. We offered our friend a room in our home if she would be Mary Poppins to our tribe while I was gone. That would allow me to be with Jodie, Ben to work and all our kids to be well cared for. She agreed. I cried. And Ben moved his office into our bedroom so she could have her own room above the garage.

* * * * * *

On January 1, the boys' orphanage posted a picture of the "twins" together. Jackson was helping Noel learn how to walk. It was a prophetic picture of the new thing God wanted us to do. He was helping us learn to walk in new neighborhoods of greater faith, leaning into Him. The entire process, I'd go back and draw strength from this photo from time to time.

Also going on in February was a whole lot of spiritual warfare over our pursuit of Jackson and Noel. We expected opposition, but not from where it came from—a few very vocal missionaries. I received many private messages all saying the same thing—we were breaking Tanzanian law. Stop. Don't do it. Tanzania's child welfare laws were rewritten several years ago. They state that a non-Tanzanian family could only adopt from Tanzania if they lived there for three years (a residency law). They also state that that requirement could be waived by the High Court if it was in the best interest of the child. The Tanzanian lawyer handling these international adoptions, and many of these missionaries' adoptions as well I might add, had successfully argued away the residency requirement for a few families from European countries because it was in the best interest of a few particular children. He believed that the trend would continue despite a lottery of five judges who heard adoption cases who might or might not interpret the law the same way. The women who rose up against us and other families in this pioneer program said that this was not the case and the residency requirement could not be waived. The lawyer and some of the judges however were arguing and ruling differently.

We didn't really know what to think, but we trusted that God would open the doors we were supposed to walk through and shut tight the doors that were against His will. We only desired obedience to Him. International adoption again after fourteen adoptions was definitely not our idea. We knew we were following Him however and if He wanted us to turn around, He would make it clear. We were partnered with Him regarding these boys for His grand purpose, and faith said that we didn't need to know what it was. We had a certain blind faith that I'm sure the Lord was counting on as He was working behind the scenes. Thankfully, I had Jodie to keep me busy while He did so.

Chapter Five

Hope

*Hope: The joyful expectation of something good
(sometimes at the end of a very dark tunnel).*

On March 3, 2015, Jodie and I flew to the Cancer Treatment Centers of America (CTCA) in Zion, Illinois, for a second opinion. So many things about the center impressed us, such as the paid for airfare for the evaluation, the limo ride from the airport to the hospital, the discounted accommodations, the whole-person approach to healing (including wonderful chaplains), the organic/healthier options cafeteria, the history of the hospital, and the friendliness of every single person we encountered. The difference in the atmosphere from Jodie's first hospital and this was night and day; black and white. I once heard someone say that the center "sells hope." They do indeed, and they do it well. In fact, that first night there during dinner, a Korean woman played guitar for us and the other guests. She sang Christian songs including "Amazing Grace." We wept. We were right where we were supposed to be, in the center of hope. Thank you, God.

The next two days, Jodie met with various departments and underwent a lot of testing to gather a current and accurate assessment of her situation. After her CAT scan, she told me that while she was undergoing it, the song "God's Not Dead" was playing in the room. Amen! He wasn't dead. There was a war going on in Jodie's body, but He was still roaring on the inside too. It was a great reminder of His love and faithfulness to both of us. By this time, the tumor was growing very aggressively, and Jodie was doubled over in pain much of those testing days, despite strong pain medication. The pain was in her left pelvic region. We had no idea just how big and severe it was until we sat with her oncologist and the surgeon to discuss the results.

They told us that the tumor was contained to that left area, but it was twisted among various organs. They believed, however, that they could do a radical surgery called a pelvic exenteration, where they would remove all the organs from her pelvic cavity. She had already had her uterus removed the summer before, but this procedure would include additional organs such as her bladder, urethra, vagina, rectum, part of her colon, and anus. It would leave her with two bags, which

Jodie called her pee and poop bags—she was always a simple sort of person. When they gave us the news, she took off her glasses, put her hand on her thin, bald head, and bent over on the exam table in disbelief that this was what hope would entail. It was more costly than she had ever imagined, but for her kids she'd lay herself down. After further discussion of the risks involved and the possibility of the tumor being wrapped around the iliac artery (in which case they wouldn't be able to proceed and would close her up), they suggested that we go to the emergency room to get the pain under control. Surgery would be scheduled for early April after she underwent a few weeks of intravenous nutrition. She was so severely malnourished that she physically could not come through such huge surgery without TPN first (Total Parenteral Nutrition).

Jodie was admitted that afternoon, and our three-day evaluation turned into a ten-day hospital stay for pain management. I had never been away from my kids that long in my life, but the Lord was teaching me something through this as well. I needed to lay my kids down on the altar and go where He had sent me. He had them.

On April 6, Jodie kissed her son, daughter, and our parents goodbye as we drove to Chicago for a radical surgery in an attempt to rid her body of cancer. On April 9, we rose early in the morning and left the hotel that we had come to love as our home away from home—it had the most comfy pillows! Surgery was scheduled for seven thirty a.m. and as we waited in the pre-op room, Jodie began to cry. I asked her why. She said she was so scared of the pain that was about to come. I climbed up on the bed, held her, then I pulled up "It Is Well" (the Bethel version) on my phone. There we lay all cuddled up on a hospital gurney and sang these words together with tears streaming down our faces. All we could do was trust in Him.

Grander earth has quaked before
Moved by the sound of His voice
Seas that are shaken and stirred
Can be calmed and broken for my regard
And through it all, through it all
My eyes are on You
And through it all, through it all
It is well
And through it all, through it all
My eyes are on You
It is well with me
Far be it from me to not believe
Even when my eyes can't see
And this mountain that's in front of me
Will be thrown into the midst of the sea
Through it all, through it all
My eyes are on You
Through it all, through it all
It is well

It is well
So let go my soul and trust in Him
The waves and wind still know His name
It is well with my soul
It is well with my soul
It is well with my soul
It is well with my soul
It is well, it is well with my soul
Through it all, through it all
My eyes are on You
Through it all, through it all
It is well with me.

I said goodbye to Jodie, and they wheeled her back. Fourteen hours later, the doctor came out to tell me that all was well. Everything went as the best-case scenario offered. Now the healing of her broken and stapled-together body needed to come.

As God was teaching me to lay everything down for Him, months before all of this I had agreed to speak at a Right to Life Rally in Wisconsin. It was scheduled to happen three days after Jodie's surgery. When we had received the date for her surgery, everything within me wanted to cancel. No one would blame me, but I knew I was being taken into yet a deeper level of surrender. When I agreed to speak, I didn't even know that CTCA existed, but God did as the rally was only a two-hour drive from the hospital. Totally doable. So I did it. I did it scared—I hate public speaking. I did it torn—I wanted to be with Jodie. But, I did it. While I was speaking on behalf of the right to life for the unborn, Jodie too had every chance at a right to life.

Jodie was released from the hospital almost three weeks after her surgery. She had much training to do with her new personal care. She had to learn a whole new way to go to the bathroom, change some eating habits because her body could no longer digest certain types of foods, and had to muster up a whole new level of strength to even sit up. Unfortunately, the pain was just as intense as she had anticipated. In the middle of her three-week stay I had gone home for a five-day break. Melissa had flown in from Florida to relieve me so I could go love on my husband and kids. I was thankful for the break, but I was also thankful to get back to Jodie. I hated for her to ever be alone and would always honor my commitment to the Lord and lay aside my own plans and comfort to make sure that didn't happen.

Chapter Six

Surrender

Jodie's big surgery and significant recovery that followed kept me too busy to obsess over what was happening in Tanzania. Ben and I had expected to make our first trip to visit the boys in March, but then April, and finally, May came, and that's when we got the green light to go meet our new sons. With that news came a whole onslaught of paperwork and childcare planning. Ben and I had never, up until this point, both left all the kids overnight in the previous eight years, let alone been out of the country at the same time. The new level of surrender to keep following the Lord down this crazy path was a level I had never known before.

Our friend staying with us during this time didn't have a job yet, so she agreed to watch eight of the kids the full eight days we'd be gone. Bless her heart. Thank you, Lord! Eight down. Another friend from church agreed to watch two of our girls and Jonathon. Bless her heart. Thank you, Lord! Three more down. That left the most concerning child, who was thirteen. He has emotional issues that you have to watch constantly as stealing, lying, and manipulation are a part of his every day. I prayed, and God answered again when a foster mom friend in Ohio agreed to watch him. Her house was set up similarly to ours because she has a child with similar needs. So two days before we were going to fly around the world, I drove him there, which ended up being a twelve-hour day in the car. It was worth it though, because he too was now in a safe place . . . and I could exhale.

Our plane left at six a.m. on May 23, 2015. The night before, several friends threw a benefit concert for us and a few other adopting families in our church. Instead of getting up at three a.m. to drive the hour to get to the airport the following morning, we headed to an airport hotel after the concert. We got a few hours of sleep before our big adventure!

We flew from Detroit to Washington, DC, and from there to Addis Ababa, Ethiopia. Ben had only been outside the country once to Korea for Benjamin's adoption. I had traveled with others for our other four Korean adoptions and to Liberia for Caleb and Madisyn's adoption. Ben isn't the best traveler, and I was a little concerned as jet lag and exhaustion seems to create illness within him, but this was God's idea, not ours, so we went with it. We boarded a huge airliner that would take us the thirteen and a half hours across the ocean to our first layover. A tangible heaviness weighed in the spirit on that plane, something I had never felt in the air before. Many of the people on board were Muslim, and many women were traveling alone with children.

About midway through the flight, I started talking to one of the young Muslim women standing with her child near the restroom, which I had gotten up to use. Small talk turned into a conversation about adoption and God's great plan for each of us. After a half hour, Ben came to look for me and found me sitting on the floor talking with this woman. I had a captive audience. I mean, where was she going to go?! I'm not sure what God did in her heart that day, but I know it was a divine appointment. She was going back to Syria for several months to visit family and had obviously thought about what adoption would be like from the questions she had asked me.

The Ethiopian airport was eye-opening for Ben and me. As soon as we got off the plane, I could feel a thick, tangible heaviness in the air. The airport was very, very crowded and predominantly Muslim. I spotted a prayer room and found myself "dying" to go into it and start saying the name "Jesus," but I reminded myself that the goal of this trip was not to be thrown in jail. Ben and I circumvented the island of shops and restaurants in the middle of the airport to find security to get to our gate, which was on the lower level. Unfortunately, we didn't realize we couldn't go back up after that point.

After we arrived at our gate, there was nothing else to do but sit and wait. The tiny chairs we sat on made it impossible to stretch out our jetlagged bodies, so the two hours before our next flight seemed more like another twelve.

After the last leg of flying, we arrived in Kilimanjaro, Tanzania, in the midafternoon. We stepped off the plane, walked down the stairs, and took in the warmth and fresh moist air as we walked across the lot into the airport. We went through the immigration line successfully, gathered our luggage, and stepped outside to a sea of brown faces holding name cards for passenger pickup. We scanned the crowd and found "Green." A man named Paul would be our driver. This was such a nice accommodation from the lawyer because we didn't speak Swahili, much less know how to drive on the opposite side of the road! We had about an hour drive to the hotel that I had booked online. I had searched diligently and read hundreds of reviews trying to find somewhere within our budget that seemed "safe" this first time. The area is one that many tourists for safaris and climbing Mount Kilimanjaro flock to, so there were plenty of hotels to choose from; but like Forrest Gump said, "You just never know what you are going to get." Thankfully, we got "amazing" this time.

On the way to the hotel, Ben fluctuated between amazement at the little shacks everywhere, the goats that walked alongside the road with the cars, the intense traffic, and . . . being car sick. Thankfully, we made it to the hotel before he actually got sick. We drove off the main paved road into a traditional village-type neighborhood and then down a winding and very bumpy road to a gated house. A guard dressed in traditional Maasai clothing opened the gate and we were warmly greeted by a man named Joseph, who eagerly grabbed our luggage and showed us to our room. We were so pleasantly surprised! The room was very Western with a comfortable bed, carpeting, and an amazing hot shower to top it off! One reason I chose this hotel was because it had a little made-to-order restaurant on site. Joseph offered to make us dinner, but we were so exhausted from the twenty-four-hour trip that we asked to take a nap first. Later that night, we went to the upper room where the dining room was and Joseph brought us an amazing made-just-for-us dinner.

The next morning after a huge breakfast of eggs, fruit plates, coffee, and lassis, our driver, Paul, picked us up and brought us to the lawyer's office, where we would go over paperwork. While we did, our lawyer, Roman, explained that there was some turmoil at the orphanage and that potential adoptive parents weren't being treated kindly or with open arms. We knew and had heard this before going there, but we also knew that God had called us to a greater assignment than just making these boys Greens. This wasn't our idea; it was His. Over the years, we had reminded ourselves of that thousands of times. Weeks prior, I had started declaring "we overcome evil with good" and we had been praying for spiritual strongholds to come down.

Isaiah 45:1-3 became a daily declaration for me.

It says:

"Thus says the Lord to his anointed, to Cyrus, whose right hand I have grasped, to subdue nations before him and to loose the belts of kings, to open doors before him that gates may not be closed:

"I will go before you and level the exalted places, I will break in pieces the doors of bronze and cut through the bars of iron, I will give you the treasures of darkness and the hoards in secret places, that you may know that it is I, the Lord, the God of Israel, who call you by your name."

God had also been setting the stage. When we announced to the world on my public Facebook page that we were pursuing these two boys, a (kind) missionary woman wrote me very excited. She and her husband were adopting a little girl from that same orphanage, and she knew our boys intimately. They were also on good terms with the management of the orphanage. So when we knew we were coming, we offered to bring supplies over for them as it's difficult for missionaries to receive things without a great financial cost attached. We had made arrangements with this sweet surrendered family to meet at the orphanage that morning after meeting Roman. When we told Roman of this "God connection" and he learned that they were at the orphanage right then, he instructed us to hurry and go. He was their lawyer as well, and he knew that this was a good thing as their family was very respected.

When we arrived at the orphanage, our missionary friends were there and they and their children greeted us warmly. We had brought two suitcases full of supplies and treats for them that they had ordered and had shipped to our house before we left. Their kids said it was better than Christmas! Little did they know that we'd come again in just a few months with their real Christmas presents we carried over from their grandparents.

They introduced us to the director and manager of the orphanage, and we stood outside in the warm Tanzanian sun and talked a bit before our friends had to leave. We took a few pictures, hugged, and hoped to meet up with them later in the week. We had arrived during the kids' naptime, and so while it ideally wasn't the best time to be there, it was God's time. It had given us a large window to share our hearts and passions with one another. We got to tell them about our family and about our passion to see all children live within a family, even the ones that we knew would die. We weren't coming to Tanzania as child collectors, as we had been accused of by the vocal few rising against us. We weren't coming on some "save the children" evangelical Christian mission. We weren't coming to break, or even challenge, laws in either country. We were there solely in obedience to the Lord. God had a special plan for these two boys—two children that had no hope or future in their birth country, but like Moses, sometimes He rescues for a greater plan. Sometimes He picks up two children out of the water of their birth country and places them in the palace because far on down the road the plan is great. Before we knew it, it was three p.m. and the boys were waking up and we were invited to go meet them.

They were more than we ever imagined.

Jackson came running over to Ben shouting, "Baba! Baba!" (Daddy, Daddy) and jumped right into his arms. Noel was calmly sitting on the floor, stimming a bit and taking it all in. He rocked back and forth, crossed his eyes and waved his hands. He was obviously more impaired than Noah back home. We had a wonderful first visit of a few hours playing with them before our driver said he had to go. We kissed them goodbye and couldn't believe all God had done that afternoon. We had so much peace and joy as we drove back to the hotel. As we walked to our room that May afternoon, Christmas music was blaring over the speakers in the hallway! "Noel! Noel!" God continued to confirm His word to us that evening through His creation as well. We walked into our room, and I opened the curtains and there, right in front of our window, were two rabbits; one white rabbit and one brown rabbit sitting side by side. I couldn't even make this stuff up if I tried! You don't need signs on a road that you travel often, but when you are on a road you've never been on, signs are a balm for your soul that you are in the middle of His will.

The next two days our driver picked us up at eight thirty a.m. and we'd arrive at the orphanage at nine a.m. We spent three hours playing with the boys and the other kids inside and outside and soaking up every detail of their little beings. This would have to carry us for some time until our court date. The orphanage is on the same road as a popular language school and so every day, the nannies walk the children down the road to play on their playground. One day, a strange man yelled for Jackson. He let go of Ben's hand and ran toward this man to be picked up. One of the nannies began yelling for Jackson to get back, and then she yelled at this man up one side and down the other. I couldn't understand a word of the Swahili she was spewing, but I knew that it had something to do with him wanting to touch Jackson, or doing something worse, for good luck. The danger of living with albinism in this country had just become real to us.

Our second to last day there, we arrived at nine a.m. as usual and I could tell something out of the ordinary was happening. The kids were being bathed and groomed extra carefully, and the nannies had clothes and shoes spread all over the laundry room. The kids were being prepped for a trip to the doctor. We were surprised when they said we could go with the kids to what was the equivalent of a well-child check here in the States. Seven toddlers, a social worker, two nannies, the manager, and Ben and I all piled into a Land Rover for the few-miles drive down the road. We pulled into a gated hospital center where we saw several old buildings and many, many people waiting outside for their turn to be seen. We drove to the very back of the complex, and the social worker got out to go and talk to the appropriate people.

Meanwhile, the kids, nannies, and Ben and I waited outside on a wooden bench outside a tiny building with peeling paint. The nannies took turns walking the kids to the back of the property line, pulling their pants down, and telling them to pee. In Africa, you wait a lot and you try again a lot. This time didn't disappoint. The social worker came back and said that they were too busy today, and we had to come back the following day. We all piled back into the *"dala dala"* as the kids called it (it means taxi in Swahili), and drove back to the orphanage. By this time it was lunch, so they stripped down the kids and put their "good clothes" in a pile for the next day when we would attempt to see the doctor again. We kissed them goodbye as our driver had arrived and was beckoning to go.

Because of our short stay and Ben's issue with car sickness, we didn't do anything touristy. We were there for the boys, period. However, I was very curious about one place, so we decided to go that afternoon. It was a large ministry set on the riverside of a coffee plantation called Shanga Shanga. They collect glass from area restaurants, crush and/or melt it, and then recycle it into things like beads and other crafts. They do more than that with handwoven fabrics and painting too, but the foundation of the ministry started with recycling something old to make it beautiful again. Not only do they do it with glass, but they do it with the people they employ. They serve as a training center and then sustainable employment for people with disabilities. They take the throwaway of Tanzania and make them useful and their lives beautiful again. This is the reason I wanted to go there of all the places we could have visited. To me, it was more beautiful than any giraffe or lion I could have seen on safari or the tallest mountain top in Africa . . . a redeemed life. It's what Jesus came to do. It's what we were there to do too.

On our last full day in Tanzania, we loaded up the kids just as the day before and attempted to see the doctor again. One very interesting thing happened during our wait this time however. A few nannies and Ben and I were all in a general-waiting-room-sort-of area outside when a very elderly man walked up to me. He had to have been at least eight-five. He wore a dusty brown suit and hat, shuffled, and carried a brown piece of paper. He told me in English that his daughter had given birth to twin granddaughters. He asked that I help name them. I didn't know what to say. It was like my brain froze because while I know hundreds of names of people back home, I had a hard time giving him any. I grabbed my pen and finally, I wrote five names of friends on the dirty folded paper he had gently put in my hand. The two names I listed at the top were Kim and Theresa. Theresa is my closest friend for over ten years, unbiological sister, and she also happens to be our pastor's wife. The nannies looked on with shock as that is never done, per them. Tanzanian men don't allow white foreigners to name their grandchildren. Now, years down the road after that event and having gone with Theresa to do ministry there several times, I often wonder if the man was an angel. The Bible says that we entertain angels unaware. Perhaps it was a prophetic moment in time where God was allowing me to seed our inheritance in this country as its people are prayed for, healed, saved, and delivered.

While the nannies gave dictation to the doctor holding terrified screaming children (it's the same in every country—kids hate the doctor!) on the scale to be measured and weighed, our driver came to take us to the lawyer. It had come time to agree in writing that these were the children we were indeed pursuing!

We went to Roman's office, where he explained in detail what the next steps would be and then suggested that we meet at the social welfare officer's office to introduce ourselves. The driver we had the last few days in Tanzania had another commitment, so he asked another friend of his to drive us. The first issue we had with our new driver was that he didn't speak English and the second issue was that he didn't know where the social welfare office was. We pulled into a gated block of rundown buildings in the shape of a U. He asked the guard where the office was and was told that it was in the back. That was about all I gathered he was told because he drove to the back and looked at all the doors and parked in the middle of the road as if to say, "Well, one of these should be it."

We waited for Roman, and waited, and waited. What was supposed to take ten minutes was close to an hour before we saw him and knew what door we were supposed to go in. He instructed us to sit on a hard, slender wooden bench in a hallway of peeling paint. Eventually, we were called into a room piled high with papers and a little man sitting behind them. Roman introduced us all, and the officer commented about my limited Swahili—apparently he thought I said one thing, which I didn't, and he thought it was cute. Roman stated that we were pursuing the adoption of Jackson and Noel, and with that the officer said, "Welcome to Tanzania. You are most welcome here." The meeting lasted less than five minutes then we were back in the car again trying to navigate the driver to our hotel as best we could with the language and navigational barriers between us.

We were set to leave for the airport the following afternoon, and we had planned on stopping by the orphanage for a short visit to say goodbye to the kids. However, Ben woke up that morning very sick. The dreaded had happened. He was sick to his stomach and lay in bed curled up all morning. We didn't eat breakfast due to Ben's stomach, and I heard something in our room of an animal nature. I was terrified to get off the bed. After an hour, I mustered up the courage to run into the bathroom and slam the door to get dressed. I then mustered up more courage to get out of the room and go ask Joseph to come and check our room for a rat or something! He was so gracious and kind and looked under the bed with a broom and in every nook and cranny while Ben lay sick in bed looking on. Joseph didn't find anything, which didn't make me feel any better as I just knew something was in there! Joseph was so concerned about Ben's obvious ill state that he asked if he could make him an African concoction that would help his stomach ache. I had been praying and Ben had been inhaling peppermint essential oil and other anti nausea medication with little success, and so he agreed.

Joseph came back a few minutes later and handed Ben a small cup of what looked like tea. Ben took a sip and nearly spit it out across the room. He said it tasted like a cup of salt.

Our driver picked us up, and we stopped at the orphanage for a short visit on the way to the airport that Sunday afternoon, May 30. Ben tried his hardest to not look sick, but he was woozy in the corner inhaling peppermint most of the time. I felt so bad for him, but at the same time, I kept telling him to suck it up. Besides, there wasn't a toilet for him to puke in as it was Saturday and the office was closed. With the grace of God, he somehow made it through the visit without being sick and we hugged and kissed the boys goodbye. It was so bittersweet. We had gotten to know their personalities that week and felt such a heart connection that to leave them was so very hard. However, there were twelve at home who were eagerly waiting for us as well.

We arrived at the airport and hurried through the necessary steps just to sit down and get a real cup of coffee at the restaurant. African (instant) coffee just was not cutting it with me anymore. I was craving real coffee so bad. We had just enough Tanzanian shillings left to buy one glorious cup of Americano. While I was sitting there trying not to be selfish and forcing myself to share it with Ben, I received an instant message. It was the director of the orphanage wishing us a safe trip home and suggesting that we stay at a cottage on the church-owned grounds next time so that we could spend more time with the boys. It was a great idea. Although the accommodations were much more rustic than the hotel, we were thankful as it saved time and money the next two times. We also decided on this trip home, that paying a little more money for the faster flight was worth it from then on.

* * * * * *

Two weeks before this trip to Tanzania, Jodie had been taken to her local emergency room with severe pain once again. She had had another CAT scan and again had heard different possible outcomes and had been admitted. Once again I had dropped everything and had driven across the state to be with her. We had heard that there was a possible abscess and the need to drain extra fluid in the region. After receiving the terminal diagnosis back in February from Dr. B, Jodie had not informed him that she had gotten another opinion, let alone had a radical surgery. So he and other medical staff were all taken aback as she updated them. Up on the floor after admission, Dr. B's physician assistant came in and told us that he was discharging her. She said there was extra fluid and that Dr. B said she could go back to Chicago and be re-evaluated there. I could hear a sting of bitterness in her tone over the fact that Jodie had done such a radical thing, and I'm sure Dr. B felt like it was done behind his back. We asked to talk to him. We couldn't believe that she'd be in such severe pain and he'd say "good luck" without even saying it to her face or examining her himself. We were given excuse after excuse as to why he wasn't coming up to see her. After two hours of waiting to confront him, we had had enough and Jodie said, "Let's get out of here. He is a coward with no bedside manner, let alone a heart."

When we were in Tanzania, Jodie flew to Chicago alone for her first post-surgery follow-up, where she received the unexpected news that there was now evidence of cancer on her liver. Not only did she receive that news, but according to the scan done two weeks prior at her local hospital, it had been present at that time too . . . and Dr. B hadn't told her and had instead discharged her without the face-to-face exam. He had kept that information from her deliberately. We were furious. He cost her more time. Just in two weeks, the two scans showed that the cancer had grown to inhabit a substantial portion of her liver. I received this news from her while she was sitting alone in a Chicago examining room and I was sitting on a bed in a Tanzanian hotel room. I hated that I wasn't there with her. For the first time during all of this, no one was there with her and that broke my heart more than the news. They wanted to start chemo that day, but she needed time to process everything. She said she needed to go home and hug her kids and then she would come back. I told her that no one would blame her for not going through with more chemo. She was still so weak from surgery and her body had been through more in two years than most people go through in a full lifetime. I will never forget what she said: "Kim, this is a new spot. I have to at least try."

And that she did. She got one round of chemo in before things took a very sudden turn.

Chapter Seven

Changing Course

In June, Jodie developed a fever. After you have a major surgery like she did, fevers are never a good thing. They instructed her to go to the local hospital emergency department again. She did everything she could to avoid going back to that hospital because of her experiences with Dr. B. She had my parents' neighbor drive her to an urgent care center rather than the hospital. It was way over their scope though and they sent her to the hospital despite her fear of another run-in with the doctor. Medical staff did lots of bloodwork and determined that she was septic. I knew this was the beginning of the end. She was not going to recover from this in the natural. She'd need a miracle to walk out of that hospital again. I arrived shortly after she was admitted into the intensive care unit (ICU). One of her friends and their mom was sitting with her until I could get there.

We had a very serious talk at that time with the doctors and the social worker. We told them that we wanted no contact or consultation with Dr. B. He was fired in our book. They respected our wishes.

Jodie spent the next three weeks in the ICU. Daily, her white blood cell counts were monitored in hopes that the antibiotics would work. Staff members were also monitoring other blood cell counts for a safe time to take her port (an implanted catheter for chemo) out. She had had it embedded into her heart for over two years; they thought it was the source of sepsis. They weren't certain if it was from that or a possible abscess on her liver. It wasn't clear from the scans. Eventually her body started responding to the antibiotics and her counts were on the upswing. The port was removed, and she had once again overcome what seemed impossible—sepsis while fighting cancer, recovering from a major surgery, in an extremely malnourished body.

During these three weeks Jodie and I had several serious conversations. She knew that she couldn't continue on like this. The cancer on her liver was growing extremely fast, and the one round of chemo she had completed was too much for her frail body. She had missed a treatment during this time and had made the tough call to Chicago to tell them she wasn't coming back. Through tears she told me, "Kim, I don't want anyone to think I'm a quitter, but I can't do it anymore."

I assured her that no one would ever link her name with the word "quitter." She chose to go through more and further than most people ever would, myself included. We made the decision together to tell our parents and Melissa that she was choosing hospice. She was done fighting off death and just wanted to do a little more living before she left this earth.

One thing Jodie expressed over and over was that Melissa come from Florida for Father's Day that year. She said it so many times that we knew it must be important to her. She wanted to give Dad the gift of all of his girls together one last year—one last happy memory to carry him through the painful months of grieving she knew would come. Melissa quickly pulled together last-minute flights, and she and her boys flew in to fulfill this wish of Jodie's. Again, the timing worked out well for me to go home and spend time with my own family. It was easier to drive back and forth every few days than stay full time. On Father's Day, we packed a picnic and everyone went up to the hospital. It had an outdoor rooftop patio, and Jodie was well enough at that point that they allowed us to push her up there with all her poles of medications. We were quite the sight strolling through the hallways and trying to fit on elevators as Jodie, Mom, and Dad were all in wheelchairs! We had a simple picnic and took what would be the last family photo on this side of heaven— Mom, Dad, and the three girls they raised.

The following week we interviewed hospices and chose one that we all felt comfortable with. One thing that particularly piqued my attention was that it was the only one in the area with a facility. I knew that another trip to Tanzania was in the future and that Melissa wouldn't be able to be in Michigan during that time. My parents were Jodie's lifeline for caring for her kids, but she was going to need some full-time care ahead that they just couldn't physically provide. It turned out to be a perfect fit for what God had allowed me to foresee. At the end of June, Jodie was discharged from the hospital and Melissa was there to help her transition to home with hospice support.

Back in March when it had become evident that Jodie was going to have surgery, she realized that she either had to move back in with our parents or move closer to them. The year prior, they had moved into a small apartment and there really wasn't room for Jodie there like she had had during the first round of chemo and radiation. God cares about every single detail though and while she was lying in a hospital bed in Chicago getting her pain managed in March, He opened up a two-bedroom apartment two doors down from my parents. Jodie would be so close that she could literally throw a stone (or spit if you are one of my sons!). Her friends and Mom and Dad moved her things out of the duplex into this small God-ordained apartment in April when she was in Chicago recovering from surgery. So, when she was discharged from the ICU into hospice in June, she was able to go to her own home. My parents were two doors down, and her son and daughter ran back and forth all day—and night.

Chapter Eight

Bucket List

When Jodie decided to stop fighting and start living out each day, she made a bucket list. Specifically, she noted all the things she wanted to do or places she wanted to experience with her kids. She wanted to leave memories, good ones. She also had a lot of things to do to bring closure so she could go to heaven in peace and without regret. That's the ironic thing about cancer at this stage: the gift of time to get things done to bring closure. If you die in a car accident or have a heart attack, you aren't afforded that gift. Jodie chose to unwrap it and leave no regrets. She had Mom and me take care of several paperwork issues; we visited the funeral home so she could have exactly what she wanted; she chose songs for her funeral and even bought the dress she was going to wear in the casket. She made peace with her ex-husband and talked about the future for their children. She forgave people that she needed to forgive, and she said sorry to the ones she had offended.

July became such a gift from the Lord. When Jodie entered hospice, staff gave her continuous morphine and another medication that for the first time in two years stopped the nausea. She actually ate like a horse for that one month! She felt good enough most days to do a little something, even if it was just sitting outside in the sun and watch the kids play. Our pastor, Pat, and his wife, Theresa, also drove across the state one afternoon to take communion with her and pray. Although Jodie didn't receive her healing, I believe that remembering the suffering the Lord took on our behalf gave her strength to live every moment left that she was given.

On Jodie's bucket list were things like visiting their favorite hot dog place and the ice cream shop that our parents took us to when we were little girls. The kids really wanted to go horseback riding and so one Saturday, I drove out for the day for that adventure with them. They had fun, Jodie soaked in their laughter, and I survived my first ride. We texted each other the next day that our butts were pretty sore!

Jodie was able to print all the pictures from her phone for the kids. They watched old videos and laughed as they remembered the good times. She wanted to leave each of them with something special and so Breyon was given a personalized wooden bat and Jasmine, a charm bracelet.

She had two big trips on her bucket list: a trip to Chicago to see Navy Pier and the Shedd Aquarium and to take the kids to Niagara Falls. The latter never happened, but Chicago did. An old friend of Jodie's gifted me the money to take her and the kids for the weekend to do everything she wanted.

Jodie and our son Noah have always had a close bond. She called him her "little buddy." He loved "Dodo" as well. I decided to make the trip extra special, so I took him along on the trip too. Her face lit up when he got out of the car with me and ran across the yard to give her a big hug. The five of us stayed at a wonderful hotel about a half an hour outside the city. The first night we went to the Pier and had dinner, rode the Ferris wheel and swings, ate ice cream, and took pictures.

We spent the following day at the aquarium. We pushed a wheelchair and stroller all day and managed to see it all and even a show. We drove back to the hotel, where we all took a much needed nap and then went back down to the Pier for dinner and fireworks. While we were waiting to be seated, Jasmine and Jodie both got henna tattoos. Jasmine's said "faithful" and Jodie's said "courage." So perfect.

One very memorable part of that trip were the breakfasts. The hotel breakfasts were crazy expensive and nothing thrilling, so we drove around a bit and found the cutest diner that served the biggest, freshest breakfasts! Each morning, Jodie ordered their huge waffle with strawberries and whipped cream. Her appetite after not eating more than a bird would for two years was gifted back to her in July. She was able to enjoy food, and she was sure to let you know it too!

The day after this big weekend away, Jodie went downhill and never really recovered. She would tell me often that she felt better when I was just there with her. On the way back to the hotel one night in Chicago, she even realized her morphine pump wasn't working and she was shocked that she wasn't in excruciating pain. It made it so hard to leave each time knowing that somehow the life I carried within me somehow strengthened her. Maybe that's why I would always go be with her whenever there was a downturn. I knew I could pull her back up to a certain point. Ecclesiastes 4:9-10 in the NLT says, "Two people are better off than one, for they can help each other succeed. If one person falls, the other one can reach out and help. But someone who falls alone is in real trouble." If love and devotion could have saved her, she'd still be here.

Chapter Nine

Goodbyes and See You Laters

The first week in August Jodie experienced many ups and downs, new pains, and returning old symptoms. Many more calls to the hospice nurse were made. She was having hallucinations and a painful time breathing when they admitted her into the hospice facility that I had counted on from the beginning. They thought perhaps she had pneumonia, but it wasn't that. They kept her there because her pain was not controlled at all and she started throwing up most meals again. Her month of a full tummy and satisfying tastes came to a halt with the turn of the calendar.

Ben and I were due to leave again for Tanzania on August 19. A week before that a conference call between my sisters, Mom, the social worker, and nurse took place. The professionals said that they could send Jodie home if she had full-time care or she could stay there longer. Insurance wouldn't pay for a full-time aide at home and although our parents lived two doors down, they weren't physically able to take on such a huge responsibility. I reminded Jodie that I was leaving for Tanzania and would be gone for ten days. I wouldn't be able to be there at all, and I was concerned about that. Jodie said very businesslike, "I forgot about that. Okay, yes. I am staying here. Thanks for reminding me about that." And that was that.

I made trips to visit Jodie every couple days and would often spend the night with her. My mom and dad were up several times in those three weeks as well as a host of friends and distant relatives who lived in town, Jasmine and Breyon, of course, and even Jodie's ex-husband. During that time, Jodie also received her twenty-year award from her workplace, Alticor, which she proudly displayed on her hospice room nightstand. It was one of the dates she was living for, and she saw it come to pass.

Four days before we left for Tanzania again, I spent the night with Jodie one last time. That morning, I helped her get some leggings and a bright pink shirt on and took her outside for the first time in weeks- and what turned out to be the very last time. She was in so much pain though sitting up that we only enjoyed the warm humid morning for fifteen minutes. I wheeled her back to her room and helped her get back in bed. A second cousin stopped by to visit, and we talked while Jodie was in and out of the conversation. I had hoped that as the time neared for me to leave that we'd be alone. I had no idea if it would be the last time I ever saw Jodie on this side of heaven or not. I thought it would be and I really wanted to say goodbye alone, but we weren't. So, I climbed on her bed and hugged her and told her that she better be here when I got back on the twenty-ninth. She said, "I will be. No broken promises." I repeated her statement back to her and gave her one last gentle tear-filled hug. I looked back as I was walking out of the room to freeze that image in my mind. I thought for sure that would be the last time I'd ever see her. She was so frail, no longer able to text or put together many coherent sentences, and in so much pain as cancer raged inside her.

How much longer could one live like that?

* * * * * *

As Ben and I boarded the plane to fly around the world, the words of Jesus in Luke 9:60 echoed in my head: "Leave the dead to bury their own dead. But as for you, go and proclaim the kingdom of God." In this case, the kingdom of God was His heart for adoption. I knew we had to do this and leave it in His hands, whatever the outcome. He was asking me, "Do you trust me?" With a hard swallow and a knot in my stomach as I buckled my airplane seatbelt, I told Him I did.

What happened on that trip to Tanzania was nothing short of a nightmare. We flew a different airline this time, and every subsequent time. It cost more money, but there was only one stop and that stop was in Amsterdam. In May and June, I had had three dreams that we missed court cases. I didn't know what they meant at the time, but little did I know that God was warning me that we were going to miss our Tanzanian court date. As it turned out, we'd miss it because we were going to miss our connecting flight! You read that right. We arrived in Amsterdam to a huge airport and thought we were sitting by the correct gate. After all, the customer service woman had pointed directly to it when looking at our boarding passes and it had the same airport code (JRO) on it. One slight mix-up though cost us an unplanned night in Amsterdam and a missed court appearance. We had no idea of this mix-up until we tried to board the plane and the computer kept spitting our boarding passes out.

We were eventually sent to another desk, where the mistake was discovered. They told us to go and stand in another line and we'd have to pay extra money and book a different flight. We found the spot pointed out to us and when a tall blond Dutch woman dressed in blue asked what happened, we told her and she laughed in our faces. That was not what we needed in that very stressed-out moment.

For over an hour, we stood in a line that barely moved until I got the bright idea to just call the 1-800 number and do it that way. In the frantic moment of realizing that there weren't any more flights going out that day and that we were going to miss our nine a.m. court date the next morning, I remembered those dreams. Ah, the dreams. God KNEW this was going to happen, and more importantly, it was OKAY. He told me so we would "fear not." It was not only what it was, it was His plan. Proverbs 3:4-6 says, "Trust in the Lord with all your heart and lean not on your own understanding; in all your ways submit to him and he will make your paths straight."

The next day we arrived in Tanzania and neither of our court dates happened. A High Court judge's son had died and the entire court system was shut down for days as all the judges were attending the multiday funeral. We were there over a week and had a wonderful time spending hours with the boys each day and getting to know the director and managers on a personal level. We also got to visit another set of kind missionary friends in another city. However, a wonderful and unexpected event occurred when Jackson's birth mom traveled twelve hours by bus to meet us.

She lives in a small village where many albinos have been killed. For love's sake, she had brought Jackson to the orphanage in this bigger city so he could live. When she heard that he had the possibility to go to America and not living in an orphanage, she couldn't believe it and wanted to make sure she did everything she could to make that happen. She met with the lawyer, signed affidavits, and gave additional information regarding anything that could be of use. During her four-day stay, she received word that her house had been broken into and everything in it stolen. You could see the devastation on her face, yet she was willing to stay if we had wanted her to. She had risked and sacrificed so much for Jackson his whole life and we told her to go, there was no more she could do. It was all in God's hands. As a wise woman with a difficult life written on her face, she told me that anything that lasts is not easy. It must make many twists and turns to knot itself as secure in eternity. We anchored in that as the devil tried to intimidate us all.

The day before we were supposed to leave, our lawyer was putting intense pressure on us to stay and wait out the court delays. He thought we could get new dates within a week or two once the judges all came back from the funeral. I had been getting messages from my mom that as soon as we left the US, Jodie's health had plummeted. By the time we were deciding to stay or go, she hadn't eaten or had any fluids in days and was in a coma. I was literally sick to my stomach for hours—and in the bathroom—trying to discern what HE wanted me to do. I wanted to be with my family for Jodie's funeral, but if Jesus wanted me to stay for these boys, "God give me peace!" I had no peace until I decided to leave Tanzania and let the lawyer be upset. I needed to be with my family and if, by God's grace, I got to kiss Jodie's bony skeleton of a face one more time, I'd be oh so thankful.

We boarded the plane the next morning, leaving two pieces of our heart in Africa knowing that we were flying home to bury another piece. The twenty-one-hour trip felt like 100 hours, and I found myself buying wooden purple tulips in Amsterdam and writing Jodie's obituary on the plane. After we landed in the US and were going through customs, my phone started loading, after having been turned off for almost a day, and began blowing up with texts and voicemails from my mom to call her ASAP.

I held it together though the interrogation part of moving through customs and when we got to the luggage carousel, I called my mom. She told me that Jodie had been seizing off and on for an hour or so and they wanted to give her some medication to slow her brain down and hopefully stop the seizures. The danger in doing so was that they thought it might slow her down to the point where she just stopped breathing. My mom didn't want to see her seize, but she didn't want me not to have the opportunity to say goodbye when she knew I'd be landing so soon. I told her to let Jodie receive the medicine but before she did, to please hold the phone up to her ear. In front of hundreds of passengers gathering their suitcases I sobbed out, "It's okay, Jodie. You kept your promise. I'm home. You can go now. I'm still coming as fast as I can, but if you go before I get there, it's okay. No broken promises. No broken promises. I love you." I hung up and ran into the bathroom, where I locked myself in a stall to sob even harder and try to pull myself together.

Friends picked us up from the airport and I was silent the whole way home. *Please, God. Just five more minutes with her before eternity.* They drove us the hour to our house. I ran inside, kissed all my kids that I hadn't seen in ten days, and hopped in the car. I hadn't slept in thirty hours and now had a two-hour trip across the state, alone. The whole drive, I kept praising Him for keeping her alive for six days without any food and four now without water. That right there was a miracle and worthy of praise! Jodie was always known for being extremely stubborn and bullheaded, and she lived that way until her very last breath. I asked him for "just five minutes to say one more goodbye" the whole drive. I pulled into the hospice facility and as I was walking in, my mom called and said, "Hurry!" I ran down the hallway and into Jodie's room, the last on the left. God not only allowed her to keep her promise to me, but He exceeded my request for just five more minutes by two hours. He is a good Father, and He gives good gifts.

Jodie died surrounded by me, my mom, a great aunt, and two of her friends. We had sung the song "It Is Well with My Soul" so many times the previous nine months and so it was fitting that as that song played, her heart stopped beating on this earth around nine thirty p.m. August 29, 2015. Although we were filled with sadness, gratefulness overwhelmed our hearts and it was truly well with our souls.

Mom and I sat alone in the room for a few moments staring, across Jodie's shell of a body, at each other in silence. Both grief and relief filled us. We each made a few fast phone calls before leaving her room. Mom called my dad and Melissa. I called Ben, Theresa, and Pat.

While we were sitting and talking for those last two hours, Mom had recalled the fleece frog pillow that Jodie had received as a gift. She recounted how Breyon really had become attached to it for some reason and it gave him comfort. I told her, "You know what 'frog' stands for, Mom? Fully Rely On God." She thought that was pretty neat. So imagine both of our surprise when we saw a frog hop in front of us as we got out of the car in front of Mom's apartment a half hour after Jodie's passing. God is always present and speaking to us through His creation.

I'd been up thirty-five hours, flown across the world, and watched my sister die. It was time for a hot American shower, a bed, and a new day.

Chapter Ten

Victory and Defeat

September through November brought another wave of change learning how to live without Jodie. After her celebration of life, her apartment was packed up, death certificates handed out, bills paid, her kids moved into a new house with their dad and stepmom, and memories were preserved. My mom, who had been frozen by the fear of cancer, came to visit our family for an extended time as well. She hadn't made the two-hour trip to visit us that I had made at least fifty times in two and a half years for fear that Jodie or her kids might need her. Mom's life had once again been resuscitated. She learned how to breathe again.

On the Tanzania front, the way things were being processed in High Court changed. Immediately after our missed flight and court dates, officials started processing all adoptions as guardianships. These three fall months brought more attempts at sabotaging God's purpose for these boys and our obedience. Thankfully, manipulation and fear are not tactics we bow to. The first attempt came when a reporter for a large Christian magazine contacted me. She explained that she had heard of our family through a previous local interview from a few years earlier and that she'd like to interview us for an upcoming Adoption Month article. We had been interviewed many times in the years past, so while the timing was horrible—two weeks after Jodie died—I agreed. A few days later, we set up a time to talk by phone. As I was standing in our laundry room, the only quiet room in the house at the time, answering her questions, I could feel the enemy at work. Her questions changed from the typical adoption type to a heavy slant on our Tanzanian pursuit. She was asking them in a way that told me I was being baited; this was not an innocent interview.

I ended the interview and sent an email immediately after stating that anything printed needed my review. I was told that that would not be possible. So they ran this story on questionable African adoptions that included parts of our story and others' stories. The funny part: I found out that the person who caused the writer to contact me was a woman who had repeatedly tried to do what she could to stop the boys (and other children) from coming to America. In November, they ran the story with some of our information but her family's pictures. It was so bizarre and done in so much darkness. It was truly a disgrace to the name of Christian publishing. God protects the righteous though, and no one seemily saw it nor did it change any dynamics, for better or worse.

During these months, the lawyer was playing cat and mouse with our agency. Our agency would ask when our rescheduled court date was and get excuse after excuse about why the dates weren't being made. Although we knew we had made the right decision, we also knew our lawyer was upset that we had left Tanzania and didn't wait out court dates as he suggested back in August. During this time we told him that we were available any time except the first week of December. Our son Isaiah was having major cleft repair surgery, and we were unavailable to leave the country during that ONE week.

You have probably caught on by now, but the delay after delay in September and October brought a middle of November announcement that our court date had been scheduled on the ONE day we asked it not be, the very date of Isaiah's surgery. Sometimes the devil is so obvious that there is no proper behavior except to roll your eyes and say, "I see you." We again had to make a decision in wisdom. We decided to push back Isaiah's surgery and fly to Tanzania for both court dates. This needed to be over with.

Our arrival to Tanzania this time around started with being stranded at the airport without transportation to the orphanage at nine p.m. in the pitch-black African night. The driver we'd had on the other two trips was, mysteriously, not there despite the fact we had been told he would be. Thankfully we had his phone number from previous times, so we asked some random Tanzanian man if we could use his phone to make a call. When we reached our old driver, he sounded surprised and said he got the time wrong—which was a lie, as all the KLM flights come in at the same time. Thankfully though, he asked us to hand the phone to another random taxi driver who was standing by and, on our behalf, he negotiated a fee with this driver and told the man where we needed to go. So because we had no other option, we got in a taxi with a stranger and trusted that he was going to take us to the baby home and not rob us and leave us stranded somewhere.

Everything turned out fine and we were safely delivered to where we were staying late that evening. No weapon formed against us ever seemed to truly prosper.

The next morning, we visited with the boys and talked with the social worker. We were told multiple times that the lawyer was not able to reach Jackson's birth mom for court with either phone number we had given him. We passed this news on to the social worker, who also knew the truth wasn't being told and made one call to Mama Jackson to tell her we were in the country and court was in less than twenty-four hours. Soon, she was on a bus to make the twelve-hour all-night bus ride across the country to make it for court. The next morning, we walked into the orphanage at seven fifteen a.m. not knowing that she had already arrived. She was in the nanny's bathroom and had apparently taken a shower. We were standing in the narrow hallway when she came out and saw us. She dropped her bag and, only covered with a thin piece of fabric wrapped around her middle, ran down the hall and hugged me and cried. She then hugged a very horrified Ben as this sopping wet almost-naked woman was lifting him off the ground with tears of joy! It was a welcome neither of us will ever forget. Trust me.

We quickly dressed the boys up in their three-piece suits and bow ties we had brought and their first pair of light-up shoes. Oh the shoes! They stomped their little feet, and all their little friends laughed and laughed. The simple joy of something they had never seen before filled our hearts.

We arrived at the courthouse at eight thirty a.m. Our court date was the same date (different judge) as the orphanage's Australian manager's adoption date, so we had someone familiar to wait with. However, waiting with two three-year-olds for three hours in the presence of AK-47s and in the midst of a very stressful atmosphere stretched us pretty thin. Thankfully, we had snacks in our bags that we stretched out as long as possible. During this time, our lawyer arrived and was apologetic for the mix-up at the airport less than forty-eight hours before. We almost believed him. His expression when he realized that Jackson's birth mom was there for court that morning though—priceless.

God certainly had our back despite his best attempts to sabotage something he had initiated. Finally, at eleven thirty a.m., we were called into a different building where we waited for an additional forty-five minutes before being called into the judge's room.

Ben, I, Jackson, Noel, Jackson's birth mom, the lawyer, and the social worker joined the judge and three other court employees in a small, hot room packed with books and furniture. Ben, I, the social worker, Jackson's birth mom, and the boys sat on two couches, and everyone else sat in chairs around a thick wooden table. The lawyer proceeded to introduce us. The judge, a woman of at least sixty, wore a hijab around her head and had the sternest look you've ever seen on a withered face. She peered over her glasses at me and asked me a few questions. I tried to defer to the lawyer as I was terrified of her, but she rebuked me sharply and told me to answer the questions, to which I did the best I could. I was thinking, *No way on God's green earth is this woman being bribed as the missionaries had accused us of. She is mean!*

The lawyer continued to state his case and word by word the judge transcribed everything he said, herself. We weren't in America anymore with the luxuries of courtroom microphones and court reporters. The room had to be absolutely silent as the judge wrote every letter of every word the lawyer said on paper in front of her. Several times, we were told to keep the boys silent, and then the first removal happened. The judge sharply told the social worker to take

Jackson out of the courtroom. It wasn't long after that that I too was told to leave with Noel.

So the driver, the social worker, Jackson, Noel, and I were all sitting in the car while the court proceeding continued inside without us. After about a half hour, I was told to go back in with Jackson as the judge had more questions. I didn't know, however, that the social worker had given Jackson her very red lipstick and he carried it in to court with him. We were ushered back into the room, where I stood next to Jackson's birth mom, who was standing and being asked questions by the judge. I had Jackson on my left hip, and I was frozen in deep concentration trying to pick up as much of the Swahili conversation that was going on. I admittedly was not paying attention to what Jackson was doing on my hip. Suddenly, the judge gasped with an expression of horror as she pointed to Jackson. I looked at him. His entire mouth was red! It looked like blood but was only the lipstick. Thank God! I explained it was the social worker's lipstick, and for the first time I finally saw the judge crack a smile. She was human after all.

We walked out of the judge's room about an hour and a half later. She told our lawyer she'd have a verdict in two months. Yes, we had to wait until February to hear what she had decided regarding guardianship. We had been pursuing Jackson and Noel for over a year and were used to waiting for every step forward, but we really didn't think we'd have to wait another two months just to hear yes or no. Like everything else though, it was another situation of hurry up and wait.

Thankfully the holidays kept us busy, but I know where they got the saying, "slower than molasses in January." Every day seemed like a week. Finally, on February 10, 2016, we received the news from Tanzania that the judge had said YES! The High Court of Tanzania had granted us official guardianship of Jackson and Noel. Nothing is impossible with God.

I'm going to skim through the next two stagnant years of this story to get to the good part. But let me share some highlights of those quiet years. After receiving paperwork and birth certificates, we filed with US Immigration in the summer of 2016. We were so very hopeful that the end of the road was in sight, but we were so very wrong. On the one-year anniversary of Jodie's death, August 29, 2016, we received written notice from US Immigration that our visa applications for the boys were both denied. This devastated us. Not only had we been denied, but we received the news on an already sad and heavy day. I locked myself in our bedroom and called Theresa to cry. We talked and she prayed over me. Another family from our agency submitted the exact same paperwork at the same time, but a different immigration officer ruled to give them their child's visa while ours got rejected. It didn't seem fair. Ben and I continued to pray and ask God if there was any other way He would have us go.

A few days later, our agency suggested we talk with a specialized immigration attorney to file for humanitarian parole. The US lawyer assured us that both children would qualify due to Jackson's albinism and Noel having Down syndrome. Her fees were another $3,000 total to gather the paperwork and file it for us. Another family in our church so graciously gave us this entire amount. They believed in us as much as we believed in the Lord's word to us. We wrote the necessary emails and waited for more paperwork from Tanzania and finally, on March 2, 2017, humanitarian parole applications were filed for both boys. The US lawyer was just as untrustworthy as the Tanzanian lawyer though, and communication and information was scarce. More waiting brought us to May, when we received a rejection letter stating that our US lawyer didn't file a fee waiver; nor did she collect the fees. She just omitted a part of the whole application we paid her $3,000 to file. We were so angry with her. She was supposed to be a specialized attorney who did this sort of thing for a living yet there had been so many slipups like this along the way. We submitted our tax returns yet again, she refiled the paperwork, and we started the waiting all over. In October 2017, we received, yet again, two more unexpected rejection notices for the boys' entrance into the United States of America. Was God officially shutting the door? Why would He grant us guardianship and make us responsible for these children's well-being if He didn't intend to let them come home to us? We just didn't understand. Now what?

Chapter Eleven

God's Perfect Plan
All Along

November and December brought several back-and-forth messages between me and the new orphanage manager, Philip. They had been more than gracious by waiting this out with us for three inconceivable years and allowing the boys to stay far past "baby age" than the orphanage accommodates. Now that we had received a second rejection of their admission to the US, we needed a new plan. This wasn't fair to anyone to keep them there. We had been paying for their care, had just started sending them to school, and so on, but it wasn't the care of a family and we knew that. It's what we wanted for them despite us not being able to bring them home. What do you do when you are legal guardians of two six-year-old boys and your country forbids you to bring them into the country? You pray continuously and ask, "Now what? We are listening."

In December, I remembered an offer that was made at least a year and a half before. A family and business owner in Canada had contacted me and said they wanted to donate their airline miles to buy our tickets home with the boys— back when we thought we were bringing them home to America. We were no longer going to bring them home, but I knew we needed to fly to Tanzania to make a new plan for them in person. I explained this and asked if by chance the offer was still open as we didn't have the funds to make the trip. They graciously said yes! They agreed to donate two round-trip airline tickets so that we could bring closure and find a permanent in-country plan for the boys.

We knew this wasn't going to be a trip Ben would go on for a few reasons, but the main one was that there was going to be a lot of driving this time. In America, Ben doesn't do well as a passenger. In Tanzania, he *definitely* does not do well as a passenger! Something about driving on the opposite side of the road and sharing the road with motorcycles and goats alike makes him extra queasy! He would have spent the entire two weeks drugged up on anti nausea meds or puking. Theresa jumped at the chance to go with me, and this gracious family from Canada bought our tickets to leave three weeks later on January 18, 2018. Ben used vacation time and kept the ship afloat at home. It all worked out beautifully!

When Theresa and I boarded the plane for the eighteen-hour plane ride across the ocean, we really had no idea what God was going to do, but we both had peace and knew this was His timing. He had something wonderful planned, but He wasn't telling us just what that was and I knew it would be yet another level of trust. Both the new orphanage manager, Philip, and I had attempted to contact several orphanages for older kids in the prior weeks. The problem we both ran into, whether the contact was made in person, phone, or via email was that they were either all full, didn't take children with special needs like Down syndrome, or weren't safe enough for Jackson to live a normal life. The bigger issue in our hearts was that we wanted a place, despite the boys' differences in abilities, where they could grow up together. Frequently, staff and volunteers alike commented on their special bond. They weren't biological brothers but were what we termed "covenant" brothers, and we believe that God moved our hearts for both of them to make sure they remained covenant brothers, forever. This was even the heart's cry of Jackson's birth mom who insisted they remain together as brothers. We all had the same vision of them growing up as brothers and apparently, we were a part of that plan.

It was especially sweet to my soul that I got to make this fourth trip with Theresa, my own covenant sister. While I grew up with two younger biological sisters, the nine years of our close friendship had evolved into the strongest of sisterhoods. Like Jackson and Noel, we weren't born into the same family, but we had become family through life's circumstances and God's sovereign hand. I finally had a big sister.

One night on my third trip to Tanzania with Ben two years before—three months after Jodie died—I had a very vivid dream. I believe God told me I was going to be given another sister just as "real" as my two biological ones. In it, Jodie and I were in an urgent care type room. She had been having problems with her stomach. She was on her hands and knees up on the exam table while we were waiting for the doctor when a baby boy was delivered—I caught the boy. We were both shocked. I asked her how in the world she had gotten pregnant when she didn't have a uterus anymore. She replied, "I don't know. I guess it must have been my relationship with McCoy in the spring?" In the spring, six months after that dream, Theresa's thirty-year-old son, Joe, had died suddenly. You've probably heard the phrase "the real McCoy." It's a phrase that means something is genuine, not counterfeit. Joe was just that, genuine, and it was through the deaths of these two loved ones that true, genuine covenant relationship was sealed between Theresa and me. Likewise, it was through Noel's abandonment and Jackson's need for safety that their relationship as brothers was created in the heavens. Neither of them asked to be separated from their mothers, but through their losses, God gave them each other.

Before we left, we had arranged through Philip to have Jackson's birth mom (Mama Jackson) and one of his biological brothers come and stay for a few days. We arrived on Friday night and they arrived Wednesday afternoon and stayed three days. We arranged for them to stay with the boys' former social worker, Helen, who no longer worked there. Mama Jackson had a relationship with her, and Helen spoke both languages, which always facilitated our visits well.

When Mama Jackson walked through the orphanage gate, however, I didn't even recognize her. She had lost a lot of weight. It was apparent that she was very sick. Yet her love was still a deep well, and she came and hugged me so tight that I had to pry myself from her arms to get a good look at her!

We were in Tanzania for ten days. God had ten days to show us what His plan was, and we were as anxious to know what it was as anyone else! Theresa said the first night that were to be like feathers and we'd float wherever the wind blew us. The first morning we woke up there we found two feathers inside the apartment by the (shut) front door. We looked at each other and knew God was winking at us. With that peace we investigated every possibility those ten days. There were six He ran past us total. The first option was Philip and his family.

As much as we loved them and would have been fine with this option, it became evident that they led too busy of a life and just didn't have the time, even if they had the right heart.

A second option came before us: a former retired nanny. She had taken guardianship of three special needs children and lived nearby, so we made a call and went to visit her. She lived in a beautiful neighborhood and humble gated home. She opened the gate, and her sweet spirit radiated from her gentle smile as she welcomed us in. Philip, Mama Jackson, Theresa, and I all sat in her living room while asking her questions about what their life would be like there. We also toured the neighborhood school they'd attend. Although the retired nanny was a beautiful woman inside and out, she was too elderly for two active six-year-old boys. I held back tears the entire visit. This wasn't home.

When we arrived back at the orphanage, Philip said that he'd review the current nannies' files. Perhaps there was one that would quit her job and become the boy's permanent caretaker in her home. The monthly stipend we were offering would cover her loss of income. A little while later, I sat in the office with Philip, the staff supervisor Elissa, and a potential nanny who was seriously contemplating the option we were presenting her with. I asked her many questions as I knew little about her. I knew it would be difficult to have a relationship with someone on the other side of the world who didn't have a computer and didn't speak the same language, but I was committed to letting God be God. He'd work those (seemingly big to me) details out if this was the door He opened. We left the meeting knowing that she would talk to her husband and we would pray.

Shortly after getting back up to our apartment, a knock came on the door. It was Elissa. She was so sweet and gentle and had simply come up to encourage me to follow peace and to remind me that God was working out all the details. Theresa and I looked at each other and mouthed "feathers." At that time, we also made plans to spend the day with Elissa that Sunday. She had invited us to go to church with her and spend the afternoon at her home. We had gratefully accepted the offer and looked forward to getting to know her and her children better.

By that evening, we were pretty tired but had agreed to walk Mama Jackson to a nearby restaurant to meet Helen, who would take her back to her house again for the night. When we arrived, Mama Jackson expressed that she did not like the retired nanny or the other potential nanny I had interviewed earlier. She gave emphatic reasons. I told her I agreed fully that the retired nanny was not a good option, and although she didn't have great reasons for the other potential nanny, I yielded in honor and said okay, we would no longer consider her as a potential caretaker either. It was then that she asked me to consider Helen. We talked further, which led to everyone's tears. Helen and I had had a three-year relationship, and although many people didn't like her, she always had served the boys and our family well. She truly did care for them, and I knew that. I agreed, and we made plans to spend the day with her the following morning. Mama Jackson was so happy. On the way out of the restaurant area, she shared with us the reason she was so weak and frail. She had contracted the human immunodeficiency virus (HIV). Theresa and I laid hands on her right there and prayed for the blood of Jesus to flow through her veins. We prayed for a miracle.

The next morning, Philip, Theresa, Mama Jackson, both boys, and I all made the hour drive to Helen's village. I had never been there before, but upon arriving we were greeted with big smiles from her, her son, and some neighborhood children and the smells from her outdoor kitchen. They had killed a chicken for us and were grilling maize to honor our visit. We entered her gated property, and she showed us her simple home. She lived in a three-room concrete block house that consisted of a living room, a bathroom, and a bedroom. She had electricity and running water and proudly showed us her new refrigerator sitting in her bedroom, where she slept with her son. She pulled cold drinks out for each one of us, and we talked further. My most obvious question was, "Where would the boys sleep?" Attached to her little house were two more cement-blocked dirt-floor rooms. One was being used for storage and the other one served as a chicken coop. She suggested some changes, including cutting a hole in the living room wall, cementing the current outside opening to the room, and laying a floor to make the chicken coop room the boy's room. Inside I was saying to myself, "Lord have mercy!" but Mama Jackson seemed so pleased that they'd have a "typical Tanzanian village life." So, I kept my mouth shut behind my pleasant facial expressions, and I just prayed.

That evening there was a meeting that was very symbolically, although not intentionally, held on a merry-go-round. In attendance were Mama Jackson, Elissa, and myself (Theresa interceded from a nearby place where she looked on). We each had concerns that we brought to the circular platform. Elissa had been friends with Helen for a long time and knew things I obviously didn't. She shared those concerns with us both. Mama Jackson shared that she also didn't fully trust Helen and was upset that Noel and Jackson couldn't go to the same school if they lived with her. My concerns were that I was leaving in two days and we were running out of time and options. It was then that we all agreed to push pause and recommit our trust in God to find a solution that we were all at peace with. With that decision, Mama Jackson decided all was well in her spirit and she would return to her home the next morning. We said very tearful goodbyes knowing that with HIV and no treatment, it might be our last. She wailed in Theresa's arms and in between sobs, spoke in Swahili of her deep love for both boys and each of us. Tears and heart-felt hugs are a universal language everyone can understand.

Sunday morning, Elissa sent friends to pick us up for church. We met her and her three children there and enjoyed an African-style tent-meeting church service. Afterward, we went to the market, picked up some fruits and vegetables, and visited a family she knew. We entered a small twelve-by-twelve mud home and to our surprise found a momma with infant triplets! Elissa helped them with milk, food, and supplies so the babies could stay with their momma versus having to surrender them to an orphanage. After our visit, we headed back to Elissa's house, where she showed us her family's land and newly built home. It was in a very safe area on a mountainside. Shortly after our arrival, she pulled us into the hallway and told us the best news we had heard on this three-year journey: "I knew the first time you walked into the office last week that I was supposed to offer to take the boys. I tried to reason and fight with God all week, but I know and have peace in my heart that if you'll let me, we will be their family." We all burst into tears and gave "thank God hugs." Peace and relief flooded my spirit. I knew we had found the boys' home. At last.

Jackson and Noel had been under the watchful eye, and governmental hand, of the Social Welfare Agency for five-plus years. Even though we were granted guardianship by the court two years before, our inability to bring them to the States had resulted in them staying in the safety of their baby home. Therefore, they also remained under the hand and gaze of social welfare up to that point.

On Monday, January 29, 2018, Philip, Theresa, Elissa, Jackson (Noel was at school), and I walked into the social welfare officer's office. Inbetween the time we had started the process and then, the office moved and the officer changed, now a young female officer was in charge of the district's children. The orphanage submitted their discharge papers, which said they were being reunited with their parents. That would be us. However, also submitted was a letter written to the social welfare agency by me explaining our immigration issues and our thought-out and agreed-upon plan to allow Elissa's family to care for them with our financial and prayer support. The social welfare officer, however, wasn't convinced that we weren't going to leave Elissa's family high and dry to care for them alone. She made us go out of her office and each write a contract to each other. Just like marriage vows, we each promised what was laid on our hearts regarding each other, keeping our future together with the boys in mind. A half hour later, we went back in now with a total of five pieces of paper.

The social welfare officer still wasn't convinced and was hesitant to give agreement. But to be completely in the clear, we needed her sign-off. We all knew that and like everything else, wanted to walk in complete integrity. I then told her, "I acknowledge what you are saying, and I realize other people may have done this and it's turned out poorly. However, no piece of paper is really going to ensure that that doesn't happen here. It's as two women before God that we are making a covenant with each other to care for them as one."

And that was that.

She signed.

Stamped it officially.

They were out of "the system."

They were set free.

The next morning, Theresa and I left for America with tears in our eyes, but with light and happy hearts. After a few preparations Elissa wanted to make, the boys left the orphanage a few days after that, together and forever. She took them home to new clothes, new schools, a father, new brothers and a sister, a bed that had been built just for them, and a permanent address.

After three years of labor pains, they finally had been given new life outside the four walls of an institution. Two families, two continents, two children and one amazing God who is the greatest storyteller of all time. Romans 8:28 in The Passion Translation says, "So we are convinced that every detail of our lives is continually woven together to fit into God's perfect plan of bringing good into our lives, for we are his lovers who have been called to fulfill his designed purpose."

Oxford Living Dictionary describes home as "a place where something flourishes" and "the finishing point in a race." Of course, I had hoped and prayed for a different final address for both Jodie and the boys, but sometimes, there is a different way home through new neighborhoods of faith. Peace comes in trusting the Lord intimately and that you are knocking on the one door Jesus stands behind. Behind that door, He is waiting to fulfill every promise. It's through the door of His kingdom that He invites you to sit at the table in agreement with Him. It's only there that you realize that even if the enemy is patrolling the neighborhood, you are dining inside the walls of the kingdom with the Prince of Peace... and it is well.

"I will place on his shoulder the key to the house of David; what he opens no one can shut, and what he shuts no one can open. I will drive him like a peg into a firm place; he will become a seat of honor for the house of his father" (Isaiah 22:22-23 NIV).

About the Author

Kim Green is the wife of 23 years to her husband, Ben, and the mother of 16 children they have adopted from around the world. With each unique adoption and such a variety of children have come many adventures and stories to share through her writing and in conversation. They attend Church on the  Street, where Kim also serves in the children's and prophetic ministries and on the leadership team. She is the author of *Enchanted Garden* published in 2018 and writes frequently on her well-followed Facebook page, His Hands His Feet Today. She is also passionate about the value of all life and has spoken for Right to Life on several occasions when she's not writing or caring for her large family. Kim currently resides in Fenton, MI.